TOM LONGBOAT

THE ONONDAGA RUNNER WHO BROKE MANY RECORDS | CANADIAN HISTORY FOR KIDS

True Canadian Heroes – Indigenous People of Canada Edition

www.ProfessorBeaver.ca

Print Edition: 9780228235286
Digital Edition: 9780228235293
Hardcover Edition: 9780228235873

Published by Speedy Publishing Canada Limited

CONTENTS

QUICK FACTS

homas Charles Longboat, who is commonly known as Tom Longboat, was born on July 4, 1886 and died on January 9, 1949. During his lifetime, he was one of the best Canadian athletes to compete in track and field events. He is most remembered for being a very good distance runner, and in particular for having incredible sprints right before he finished his races.

TRADITIONAL CHIEF OF
THE ONONDAGA NATION

Tom was Indigenous and he belonged to the Onondaga Nation.

Did you know?

ONONDAGA MEANS PEOPLE WHO KEEP THE CENTRAL FIRE OR HILL PLACE. THE MEMBERS OF THIS INDIGENOUS GROUP OF PEOPLE ARE ORIGINALLY FROM A PLACE IN THE STATE OF NEW YORK, IN THE UNITED STATES OF AMERICA (USA), JUST SOUTH OF LAKE ONTARIO.

Tom started distance racing in 1905 and he soon began to show what a gifted runner he was. He was the first Indigenous person to win the Boston Marathon. He also won many popular races in Canada. In addition, he competed in the 1908 Olympics.

He has won many races and many awards. He was inducted to both Canada's Sports Hall of Fame and Canada's Olympic Hall of Fame.

TOM LONGBOAT WITH THE WARD
MARATHON TROPHY IN 1907

TOM WAS ONE OF THE WORLD'S
BEST MARATHON RUNNERS.

In addition to being a distance racer, Tom served in the Canadian Armed Forces. He even ran while in the Armed Forces, both in the line of duty and during competitions. Tom Longboat was one of the world's best marathon runners!

Tom's Birth and Early Years

WELCOME TO

Six Nations

A 1999 Caring Community

THE ONTARIO TRILLIUM FOUNDATION
LA FONDATION TRILLIUM DE L'ONTARIO

SIX POINTS

1 EXERCISE REGULARLY

2 STOP SMOKING

Tom Longboat was born on July 4, 1886 on the Six Nations Reserve near Brantford, a city in southern Ontario.

Tom's father's name was George Longboat and his mother's name was Elizabeth Skye. George Longboat was a farmer. Tom was the middle child of three children. He had a sister, Lucy, who was older and a brother, Simon, who was younger.

Did you know?

A Reserve is an area of land on which Indigenous peoples live. It is for the exclusive (only) use of Indigenous peoples.

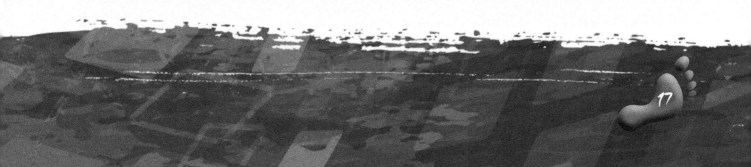

Tom was a member of the Wolf Clan who came from a group of Indigenous people known as the Onondaga Nation. They were members of what is referred to as the Iroquois Confederacy, or Haudenosaunee as they called themselves. They started out as a group of five and later became six different Indian tribes in the northern part of the state of New York.

The Indigenous name that was given to Tom was Cogwagee and in English, it means everything.

TOM SPENT HIS EARLY CHILDHOOD ON A FARM WHERE HE LOVED TO RUN.

Tom spent his early childhood on a farm where he loved to run. Tom had to do different chores on the farm. One of his responsibilities was to bring the cows back. He enjoyed running so much that he would run to get the cows!

Sometimes, his family thought that he was exaggerating about how far he could run and how fast he could get there. One day, he was finally able to convince them. He beat his brother to Hamilton, which was about twenty miles from where they were. The amazing thing is that his brother went by a horse drawn carriage whereas Tom went by foot. What is more incredible is that his brother left before Tom did!

At the age of twelve years, Tom was sent to the Mohawk Institute Residential School. At that time, Indigenous children were forced to attend a residential school by the Canadian government.

Did you know?

A Residential School was a school that was set up by the Canadian government to teach European culture and language to Indigenous children. The children were forced to give up their own language and culture and take on the European language and ways. There are no more residential schools in Canada. The last one was shut down in 1996.

MOHAWK INSTITUTE RESIDENTIAL SCHOOL

23

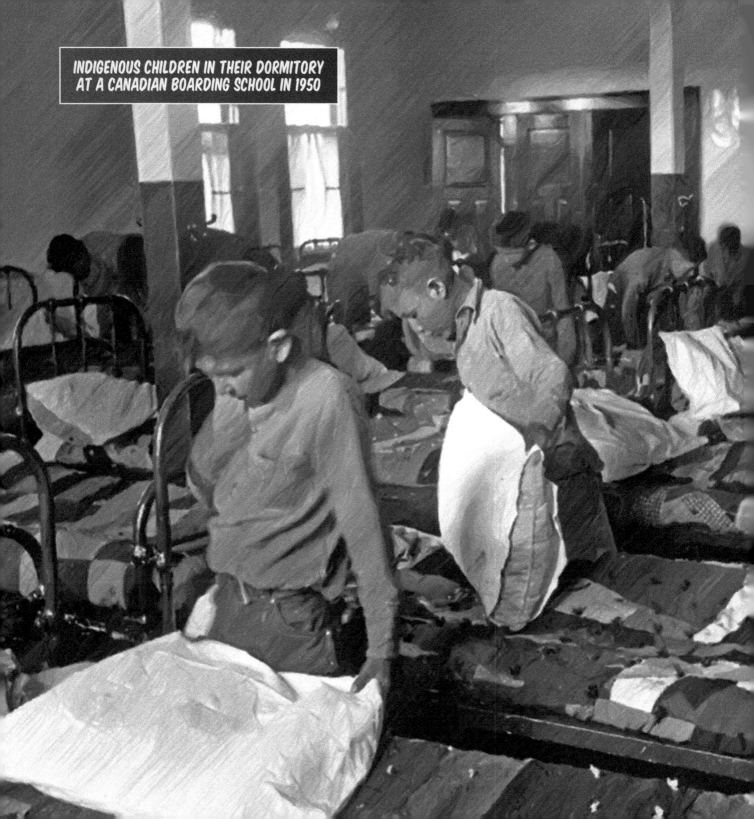

INDIGENOUS CHILDREN IN THEIR DORMITORY AT A CANADIAN BOARDING SCHOOL IN 1950

Like many Indigenous children, Tom did not like having to attend the residential school, which some referred to as the Mush Hole. He disliked it so much that he ran back home, which was approximately twelve miles away. Sadly, he was sent back to the Residential school and punished.

Despite the harsh punishment he received, Tom ran away from the school again. This time he went to one of his uncles. His uncle hid him for a while and used the time to teach Tom some Indigenous values. Tom was taught how to farm and how dedication and hard work could help him.

Tom's Career as a Distance Runner

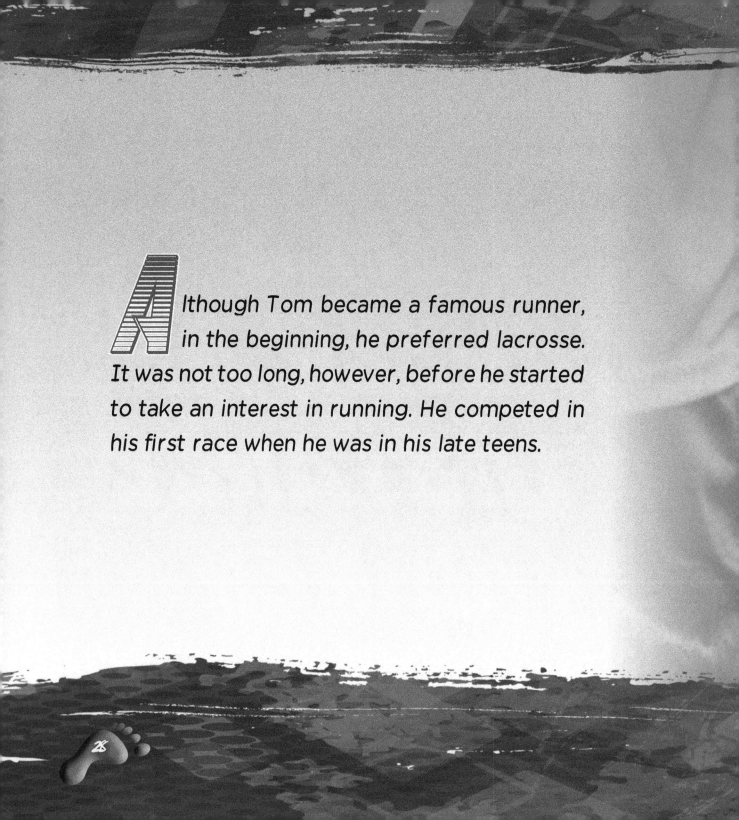

Although Tom became a famous runner, in the beginning, he preferred lacrosse. It was not too long, however, before he started to take an interest in running. He competed in his first race when he was in his late teens.

IN THE BEGINNING, TOM PREFERRED LACROSSE.

PEOPLE STARTED TO NOTICE THAT TOM WAS A GIFTED RUNNER.

He ran in the Victoria Day Race in Caledonia and came in second place. Coming second only made him work harder! He competed in the same race again and came first place!

It did not take long for people to start to notice that Tom was a gifted runner. One person who took notice was an Indigenous man by the name of Bill Davis who became Tom's coach.

Tom's coach signed him up for a race in Hamilton known as Around the Bay. The race covered an area of nineteen miles. Some of the spectators (people watching an event) put bets on who they thought would win. Not many people bet for Tom, which was unfortunate for them because he won!

RUNNERS LINED UP FOR THE HAMILTON'S AROUND THE BAY ROAD RACE

Tom went on to win many more races. For example, he won the Toronto Ward's Marathon. The newspapers started to write about him. Different news reporters started to make up different names for Tom. These names included, The Indian Iron Man, The Speedy Son of the Forest, the Streak of Bronze to Wildfire and The Running Machine.

One of the most well-known races that Tom won was the Boston Marathon on April 19, 1907. The Boston Marathon, as its name would suggest, is held every year in the city of Boston, Massachusetts in the USA.

BOSTON MARATHON FINISH LINE

At that time, the Boston Marathon was twenty-five miles in length. It is now 26.2 miles in length. Tom made a record in this event in two different ways. First of all, he was the first winner of the Boston Marathon who was Indigenous. The second thing is that he actually finished in record time! He broke the previous runner's record by a little more than five minutes. It was very impressive, especially since the weather was not good on the day of the marathon.

TOM WAS THE FIRST WINNER OF THE BOSTON MARATHON WHO WAS INDIGENOUS.

TOM RAN IN THE MEN'S MARATHON IN THE 1908 SUMMER OLYMPICS IN LONDON, ENGLAND.

In 1908, he ran in the men's marathon in the Summer Olympics that took place in London, England. Despite having won the Boston Marathon, Tom's ability as a distance runner was questioned by athletic organizations in both Canada and the USA. He was not even officially chosen to represent Canada by the Olympic committee.

Nonetheless, he entered the Olympic marathon and his travel expenses were paid by the club of which he was a member. Although Tom worked hard, he did not come first place in this event. He became overcome from exhaustion and had to quit the race. When he withdrew (quit) he was in second place and only had 6.2 miles left to get to the finish line.

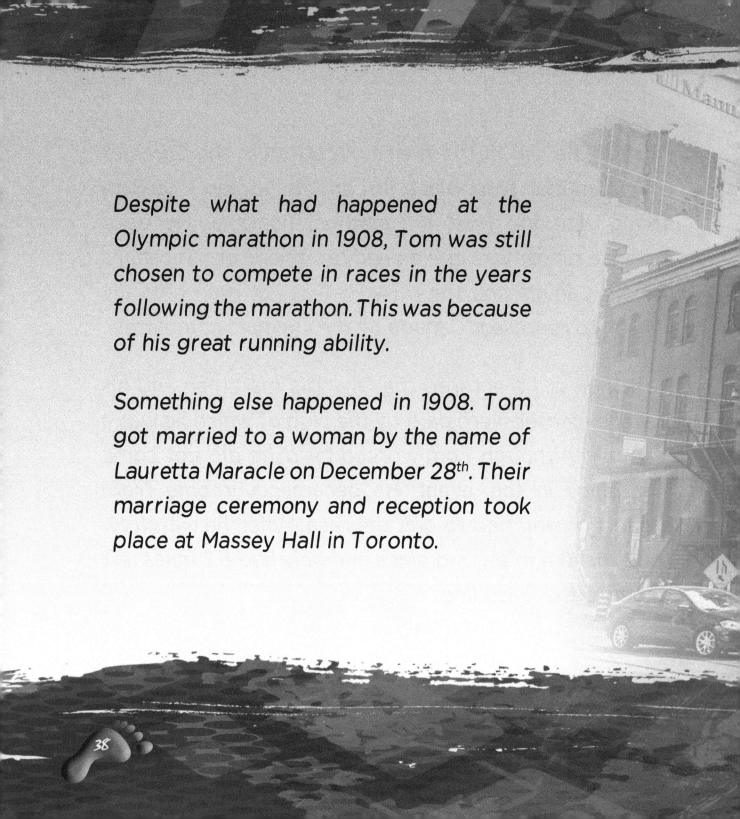

Despite what had happened at the Olympic marathon in 1908, Tom was still chosen to compete in races in the years following the marathon. This was because of his great running ability.

Something else happened in 1908. Tom got married to a woman by the name of Lauretta Maracle on December 28th. Their marriage ceremony and reception took place at Massey Hall in Toronto.

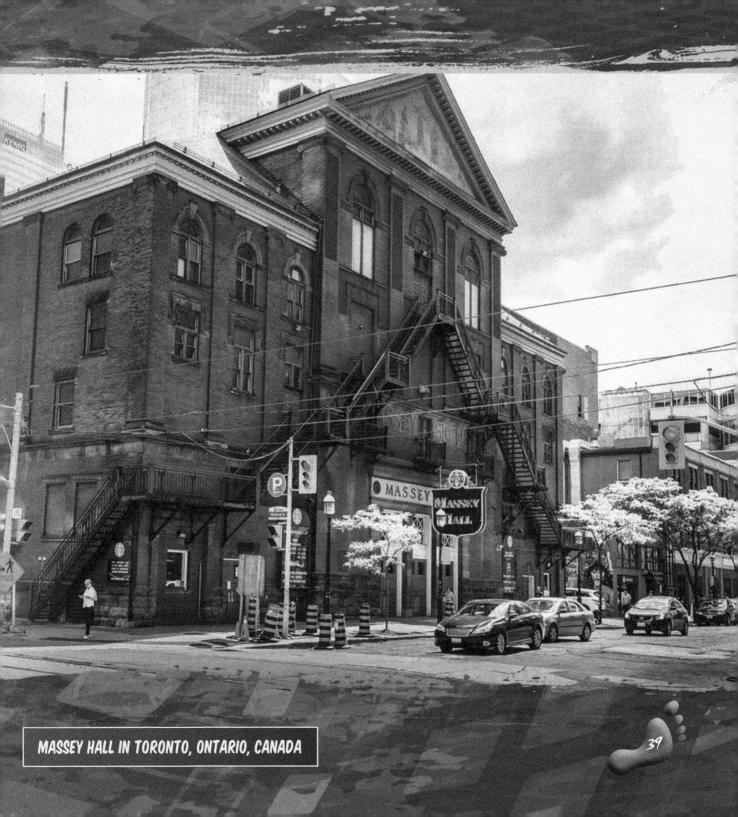

MASSEY HALL IN TORONTO, ONTARIO, CANADA

40

TOM WAS AWARDED THE TITLE
PROFESSIONAL CHAMPION OF THE WORLD.

In 1909, Tom entered the World's Professional Marathon Championship and came first place. He was awarded the title, Professional Champion of the World. It was at this point that Tom became a professional runner.

Not only did Tom go on to win more races, after turning professional and being declared a world champion, he also broke records.

Tom's Involvement in the Canadian Army

Tom served in the Canadian Army in World War One (WWI). He was a member of the 107th Pioneer Battalion. It is no surprise that his military service included running! He worked as a message carrier whose job was to dispatch (deliver) messages quickly from one military post to another. This was a very dangerous thing to do because the job put Tom at risk of being shot by a sniper (a person who hides with a rifle waiting to shoot another person) but Tom took it upon himself to serve this way. He was both loyal and brave. He did this job for four years even though he received two injuries during the war.

Not only did Tom run as a part of his job, he also entered several army competitions. In 1918, he came first place in the eight-mile event in the Dominion Day Competition.

TOM SERVED IN THE CANADIAN ARMY IN WWI AS A MESSAGE CARRIER.

Tom's Life After WWI

In 1919, Tom returned to Canada. He got quite a shock when he found out that his wife was married to someone else. It had been reported that Tom was killed in the war but this was not true.

Nevertheless, Tom accepted it. Later, he got married to Martha Silversmith who was also from Six Nations. Four children were born to them.

MARTHA SILVERSMITH

49

At this point of his life, Tom had to decide what to do next. He worked with the Veterans Guard for a while. He moved to Toronto, the capital city of the province of Ontario. He worked at a number of different jobs while he was there.

At this period, racing was no longer popular. Many people seemed to have lost interest in it as a spectacular sport.

TORONTO

NATHAN PHILLIPS SQUARE
IN DOWNTOWN TORONTO

52

Tom remained in Toronto until 1944. He then decided to return to the place of his roots, the Six Nations Reserve. He remained there for the rest of his life. On January 9, 1949, he died of pneumonia which he got as a result of complications from diabetes. He was sixty-three years old.

Tom's Honours and Awards

Tom has received a lot of recognition for his achievements in distance running.

56

THE TOM LONGBOAT AWARD IS PRESENTED TO AN INDIGENOUS PERSON WHO HAS SHOWN GREAT ATHLETIC ABILITY.

In 1951, there was an award put in place to honour him. It is called the Tom Longboat Award and it is a medallion (a circular medal that can be put on a chain and worn around a person's neck). Every year, in Canada, the award is presented to an Indigenous person who has shown great athletic ability.

THE TOM LONGBOAT MEDALLION

In 1955, he was inducted into the Indian Hall of Fame as well as Canada's Sports Hall of Fame.

CANADA'S SPORTS HALL OF FAME
IN CALGARY, ALBERTA, CANADA

In 1980, there was an athletic group established (made) and the name chosen for it was done so in Tom's honour. The group is called the Longboat Roadrunners and it is one of the largest and most popular running groups in Toronto.

THE LONGBOAT ROADRUNNERS

ONTARIO SPORTS HALL OF FAME LOGO

In 1996, Tom was inducted into the Ontario Sports Hall of Fame.

In 1999, Maclean's Magazine, a national magazine in Canada, listed him as being one of the ten most famous people.

MACLEAN'S MAGAZINE LISTED TOM AS BEING ONE OF THE TEN MOST FAMOUS PEOPLE.

In 2000, two important things happened that honoured Tom. One was that there was a Canadian postage stamp made with Tom's image on it. The other thing is that a new race called the Tom Longboat Run was created at the I.L. Thomas School, a Six Nations School.

TOM LONGBOAT STAMP

TOM LONGBOAT RUN

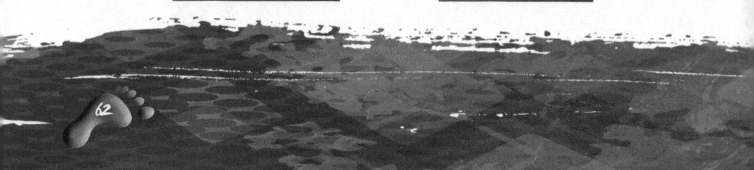

I.L. THOMAS ELEMENTARY SCHOOL
IN OHSWEKEN, ONTARIO, CANADA

63

TOM LONGBOAT DAY RACE AT SIX NATIONS OF THE GRAND RIVER

In 2004, a movie entitled, "Chiefs & Champions: Tom Longboat" was made to tell Tom's biography (life story).

In 2008, Tom had a day set aside in his honour. It is called Tom Longboat Day and it is observed every year in the province of Ontario on June 4th. The reason that it happens on June 4th instead of July 4th, which was Tom's birthday, is that there was a misunderstanding about whether he was born in June or July. However, there are records to support that he was indeed born in the month of July.

In 2015, a monument, which was given the name, "Challenge and Triumph" was made in Tom's honour. The monument was done by David M. General, a Six Nations artist, and it took him seven months to complete it. The purpose of the monument is to show different things about Tom, such as his Indigenous values, his outstanding ability to run, and his brave contribution in WWI.

TOM LONGBOAT

TOM LONGBOAT, SIX NATIONS WORLD RUNNER

CHALLENGE AND TRIUMPH
MONUMENT IN TORONTO, CANADA

HALL OF HONOUR

CITY OF SPORT

TORONTO SPORT HALL OF

TORONTO SPORT HALL OF HONOUR

In 2018, Tom was given the award the "Toronto Sport Legend" and he was inducted into the Toronto Sport Hall of Honour.

Tom can undoubtedly be considered a true Canadian hero!

Visit

www.truecanadians.ca

TRUE

to learn about other True Canadian
stories and/or view our catalogue of
edutaining children's books.

CANADIAN SERIES

Lightning Source UK Ltd.
Milton Keynes UK
UKHW050755080121
376661UK00002B/50